Kangaroos

Jill Esbaum

NATIONAL
GEOGRAPHIC
KiDS

WASHINGTON, D.C.

Boing! Boing!

What kind of animal is that, bouncing along, hippety-hop, across a sea of sandy scrubland?

It's a kangaroo!

Kangaroos wander from here to there, snacking on yummy grass.

Leaves are another tasty treat.

Munch, crunch, munch.

Snuggle!

Born the size of a grape, a baby kangaroo crawls into its mother's pouch right after it is born.

A baby kangaroo is called a joey.

Mother's pouch is warm and safe. The baby drinks her milk and grows. It pops up to peek at the world from time to time.

After a few months, the joey is big enough, brave enough, to wriggle out of the pouch.

At first, the joey sticks close to Mother. But soon, the young kangaroo is hopping all over the place.

While her joey explores, the mother kangaroo listens and watches for hungry eagles and dingoes.

She knows they like to hunt little joeys.

Hurry!

An eagle swoops low.
The mother clicks
a warning to her joey
and stomps
her huge feet.

Thump, thump!

The joey knows what that means. Quick! Back to the pouch! The joey dives in.

Whew.

A joey has a lot to learn. It keeps an eye on Mother.

She nibbles something green. The joey nibbles something green.

She scratches. The joey scratches.

Scritch, scritch, scritch.

17

Squeezing into Mother's pouch gets tougher as the joey grows.

Sometimes, not all
of him makes it inside.

Oof, those big feet!

After many months, the joey leaves its mother's pouch for good. But it still has a lot to learn ...

... like arm licking.

That's what kangaroos
do to stay cool.

Slurp, slurp!

21

Rolling in dust
or sand keeps
a kangaroo's
fur fluffy.

22

A nap in the shade feels oh so nice.

23

Hop along, roos!

Now the joey is a big strong hopper, like its mother. *Boing! Boing!*

The word "kangaroo" is often shortened to "roo."

Meet the Family

Kangaroos are marsupials. Marsupial mothers carry their babies in their built-in pouch. There are more than 60 animals in the kangaroo family. Here are just a few:

RED KANGAROOS are the largest kangaroos.

TREE KANGAROOS live in trees in rain forests.

EASTERN GRAY KANGAROOS have brownish gray fur.

ANTILOPINE KANGAROOS have shaggier fur than other kangaroos.

YELLOW-FOOTED ROCK WALLABIES leap from boulder to boulder.

27

Built for Bouncing

Its heavy tail helps a kangaroo keep its balance while hopping.

Most kinds of kangaroos have hind legs that always move together when the animal is on land. That means these kangaroos cannot walk like a person. They cannot move backward either. But they sure can hop!

Big, strong feet are perfect for pushing off from the ground.

Can you hop like a kangaroo?

28

At top speed, some kangaroos can jump forward 30 feet (9 m) per hop. That's almost the width of a tennis court!

Can you name some other animals that hop?

Tree kangaroos can move their hind legs separately and move backward. That makes it easier to climb down a tree!

A kangaroo's powerful hind legs are springy, so hopping is easy and natural.

Kangaroos are good swimmers.

Where Kangaroos Live

Kangaroos live in Australia, New Guinea, and islands nearby.

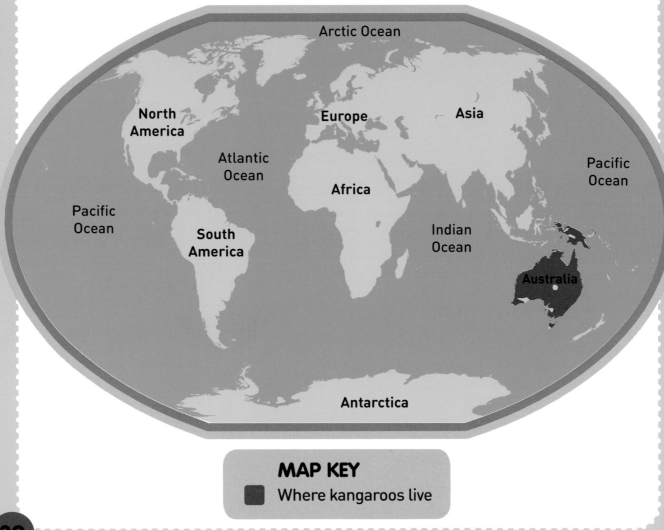

Arctic Ocean

North America

Europe

Asia

Atlantic Ocean

Pacific Ocean

Africa

Pacific Ocean

South America

Indian Ocean

Australia

Antarctica

MAP KEY

Where kangaroos live

Read the Signs

In Australia, special signs remind drivers to watch out for kangaroos crossing the road. In other places, road signs show different animals. Can you name all the animals in these signs?

1. sea turtle; 2. elephant; 3. crab; 4. sheep; 5. kangaroo; 6. deer

For Quinn Josephine —J.E.

Since 1888, the National Geographic Society has funded more than 12,000 research, exploration, and preservation projects around the world. The Society receives funds from National Geographic Partners, LLC, funded in part by your purchase. A portion of the proceeds from this book supports this vital work. To learn more, visit natgeo.com/info.

NATIONAL GEOGRAPHIC and Yellow Border Design are trademarks of the National Geographic Society, used under license.

Trade paperback ISBN: 978-1-4263-3157-2
Reinforced library binding ISBN: 978-1-4263- 3158-9

Designed by Caroline Foster

The publisher gratefully acknowledges Dr. Daniel Ramp, Director, Centre for Compassionate Conservation, University of Technology, Sydney, Australia, for his expert review of this book.

Printed in China
18/RRDS/1

ILLUSTRATIONS CREDITS

Front cover, John White Photos/Getty Images; **back cover,** Cyril Ruoso/Minden Pictures; 1, Kitch Bain/Shutterstock; 2-3, Theo Allofs/Minden Pictures; 4-5, Arco Images GmbH/Kimball Stock; 6, Bennymarty/Dreamstime; 7 (LE), Klein and Hubert/Minden Pictures; 7 (RT), Jan Pokorn/Dreamstime; 9, K.A.Willis/Shutterstock; 10, Eastcott Momatiuk/Getty Images; 11, Cyril Ruoso/Minden Pictures; 12 (UP), TerriSymons/Getty Images; 12 (LO), CraigRJD/Getty Images; 13, Yva Momatiuk and John Eastcott/Minden Pictures; 14, John Carnemolla/Shutterstock; 15 (UP), Kjuuurs/Shutterstock; 15 (LO), Yva Momatiuk and John Eastcott/Minden Pictures; 16 (LE), Juniors Bildarchiv GmbH/Alamy Stock Photo; 16 (RT), Yva Momatiuk and John Eastcott/Minden Pictures; 17, Juergen Sohns/Alamy Stock Photo; 18, K.A.Willis/Shutterstock; 19, Jean-Yves Tran/Getty Images; 20, Boy_Anupong/Getty Images; 21, fmajor/Getty Images; 22, Joe McDonald/Getty Images; 23 (UP), MB Photography/Getty Images; 23 (LO), Auscape/Getty Images; 24-25, FLPA/Alamy Stock Photo; 26 (LE), Arco Images GmbH/Alamy Stock Photo; 26 (RT), imageBROKER/Alamy Stock Photo; 27 (UP), Dennis Jacobsen/Shutterstock; 27 (LO LE), lenorehaskins/Getty Images; 27 (LO RT), Tier Und Naturfotografie J und C Sohns/Getty Images; 28-29, Rebecca Jackrel/Getty Images; 29 (LE), Theo Allofs/Minden Pictures; 29 (RT), Roland Seitre/Minden Pictures; 31 (UP LE), crisserbug/Getty Images; 31 (UP CTR), CamiloTorres/Getty Images; 31 (UP RT), cnic-bc/Getty Images; 31 (LO LE), swissmediavision/Getty Images; 31 (LO CTR), asiafoto/Getty Images; 31 (LO RT), ND700/Shutterstock; 32, bschuitdesign/Getty Images